Mel Bay Presents

Fiddling
Around the World

by Mary Ann Harbar

D0870772

CD CONTENTS

1	Jesuscita in Chihuahua	21	Fiddler's Polka	41	Bučimiš
2	Cattle in the Cane	22	Krakowiak	42	Doina
3	Blackberry Blossom	23	Ay Lučka Lučka	43	The Lark
4	Jolie Blon	24	A Ja Sam	44	Slow Hora in D Minor
5	La Bastringue	25	Tançoj Tançoj	45	7:40 A.M. [1:14]
6	La Grande Chaine	26	Ennalam Egy Boldog Ora	46	Klezmer Wedding Dance
7	St. Anne's Reel	27	Szép Assonynak	47	Kolomeyka Medley
8	Arthritica	28	Vega Vega Mar	48	Ukrainian Medley
9	Coleraine	29	Danza Piemontese	49	Kolomeyka #1
10	Dennis Murphy's Slide	30	La Quadriga	50	Musician's Polka
11	Farewell to Erin	31	Sicilian Tarantella	51	Hopak
12	Irish Polka Medley	32	Drmeš iz Ždenčine	52	Bright Shines the Moon
13	Slip Jig Medley	33	Čujes Mala	53	Karapyet
14	Tarbolton	34	Ja Sam Jovicu	54	Korobushka
15	Banks Hornpipe	35	Seljančika	55	Leyla
16	Morpeth Rant	36	Užičko	56	Aziz
17	Full-Rigged Ship	37	Hassaposérviko	57	Mustafa
18	Gardy Belotin	38	Karagouna	58	Omni
19	The Wanderer's Tune	39	Samiotissa		
20	Clarinet Polka	40	Makedonsko Devojke		

Cover photo by Rick Gardner

1 2 3 4 5 6 7 8 9 0

Visit us on the Web at www.melbay.com — E-mail us at email@melbay.com

Contents

Introduction 3
Quick Reference Key and Glossary 4

Mexican
1. Jesuscita in Chihuahua (Jesse Polka) 6

Bluegrass
2. Cattle in the Cane 9

Old-Time
3. Blackberry Blossom 10

Cajun
4. Jolie Blon 12

French Canadian
5. La Bastringue 13
6. La Grande Chaine 14
7. St. Anne's Reel 16

Cape Breton
8. Arthritica 19

Irish
9. Coleraine 20
10. Dennis Murphy's Slide 21
11. Farewell to Erin 22
12. Irish Polka Medley 24
13. Slip Jig Medley 28
14. Tarbolton 31

Scottish
15. Banks Hornpipe 32

English/Northumbrian
16. Morpeth Rant 34

Shetland
17. Full-Rigged Ship 35

Scandinavian
18. Gardy Belotin 36
19. The Wanderer's Tune 37

Polish
20. Clarinet Polka 38
21. Fiddler's Polka 40
22. Krakowiak 42

Czech
23. Ay Lučka Lučka 43
24. A Ja Sam 44

Slovak
25. Tančuj, Tančuj 45

Hungarian Czardas Medley
26. Ennalam Egy Boldog Ora 46
27. Szép Assonynak 46
28. Vega Vega Mar 48

Italian
29. Danza Piemontese 50
30. La Quadriga 52
31. Sicilian Tarantella 54

Croatian
32. Drmeš iz Zdenčine 56

Serbian Kolos
33. Čujes Mala 58
34. Ja Sam Jovicu 61
35. Seljančika 62
36. Užičko 64

Greek
37. Hassaposérviko 66
38. Karagouna 69
39. Samiotissa 70

Macedonian
40. Makedonsko Devojke 71

Bulgarian
41. Bučimiš 72

Romanian Set
42. Doina 74
43. The Lark 74

Moldavian
44. Slow Hora in D Minor 76

Klezmer
45. 7:40 A.M. 78
46. Klezmer Wedding Dance 80

Ukrainian
47. Kolomeyka Medley 81
48. Ukrainian Medley 84
49. Kolomeyka #1 86
50. Musician's Polka 88
51. Hopak 90

Russian
52. Bright Shines the Moon 92
53. Karapyet 97
54. Korobushka 100

Middle Eastern
55. Leyla 105
56. Aziz 106
57. Mustafa 107

Gypsy Style
58. Omni 108

Alphabetical Index of Tunes 110
About the Author 111

Introduction

This book is for you, the violinist/fiddler who wants to have fun expanding your repertoire and technique to include popular ethnic music. This eclectic sampler is largely accessible to the intermediate student, and we've included some harmonies for twin fiddling. The companion CD should facilitate picking up the flavors of the various styles. You can pan it to isolate the melody from the harmony or rhythm.

The tunes herein are edited to present their idiomatic ornaments, bowings, etc. in a way that's comfortable and easy to learn. Most represent hybrids of interpretations rather than that of one particular fiddler. Traditional fiddlers seldom play a passage the same way twice and will often vary the ornaments and bowings more than in these arrangements. (You'll hear subtle variations on the CD.) Once you've gotten these versions under your fingers you will have the basic building blocks to create your own embellishments, articulations, variations, and so forth.

Repeats were sometimes omitted in the recordings so we could fit all the tunes on the CD.

No notation can fully capture the nuances of a style. It's essential to listen to traditional fiddlers of each genre to absorb its feel.

Dedicated to my student Diehl Moran, who inspired this collection, and who now teaches me!

My heartfelt thanks to those who contributed to the research, arranging, editing, recording and illustration of this work:

Ann Derby - Houston Photo Imaging
Anna Golka
Barry Roberts
Charley Rappaport
Dave Peters
David Klingensmith
Diehl Moran
Doug Robertson - Citizen Doug Prod.
Eden Somer
Frances Newton
George Caba
Greg Harbar
Gregory Ballog
Jan Zollars
Janet Cook
Jim Scoggan - Violin Gallery
Joanne Dodd

Joe Compean
Joe Oberaitis
Karl Caillouet - Heights Sound Studio
Kelly Lancaster
Ken Kneszik
Laura Gibson
Lloyd Gibson
Martin Kalisky
Michael Schlesinger - Global Village
Mike Mizma
Mrs. Adam Mazewski
Pista Farkas
Rick Gardner Photography
Steve Wolownik
The Houston International Folkdancers
Turlach Boylan
Zhenya Kolykhanov

I am most indebted to my husband Greg Harbar, who taught me with love and exuberance practically everything in this volume and much, much more.

Quick Reference Key and Glossary

◼   Downbow.

V   Upbow.

(◼),(V)   Parenthesis around a bowing indicate to play it that way on the repeat of a section.

(♭),(♯),(♮)   Courtesy accidental. Parenthesis around a flat, sharp or natural sign are a reminder to resume playing that pitch as indicated by the key signature.

↑ ↓   Play the note slightly sharp or flat.

╲ , ╱   Slide your finger into or from the pitch, in the direction indicated.

╲ ╱   Slide down, then up.

{   Broken chord. Start the chord on the lower strings, then cross to the upper ones.

〜   Slide, while shaking the hand as in a wide fast vibrato.

‿ , ⌢   1. Slur. Play the included notes in the same bow.
2. Tie. Two or more notes of the same pitch played as one.

     Slur with a separation after note(s) with a dot.

     Ricochet (see explanation on tune #15)

     Slur with a semi-separation after each note with a dotted dash.

     Slur with a slight stress on each note with a dash.

♩   Staccato (on the string), spiccato (bounce the bow) or sautillé (springing bow - only the stick bounces while the hair remains in contact with the string). Depending on the tempo and style, the dot under or over a notehead indicates to play that note short, using one of these techniques. Many of the tunes in this book call for an articulated bowstroke throughout.

＞   Accent, using bow pressure and/or speed.

◁   Crescendo (pronounced "Cre-shen-do"). Increase volume as the "hairpin" opens up.

⁓   Here used to indicate a roll, as explained in the Irish section.

♪,♫   Grace note(s). Very quick note(s) (sometimes found in pairs or groups) preceding and connected to the main note.

♪♪♪ , ♩♩♩   Triplet. 1. Three notes in the space of one beat. (Same principle applies to sextuplet - six notes in the space of one beat, etc.) 2. Bowed triplet (see the Irish section).

,   Lift the bow off the string for a slight pause.

⌢   Fermata, "bird's eye." Hold the note longer.

⌐1.⌐   Ending for a section whose last bar(s) vary on the repeat(s). Play the endings as indicated for whichever time you're on.

[A]   Rehearsal letter indicating a main section.

[A']   Rehearsal letter indicating a variation of the designated section.

[A¹]   Rehearsal letter indicating one of multiple variations of a section.

⊕   Coda. A tag after the end of a song. If you see the two coda symbols, jump from the first to the second the last time through the song, to end the song.

8va	An octave higher.
ad lib	*Ad libitum,* "at pleasure." Interpret this passage as you please.
arco	Resume playing with the bow (after *pizzicato* section).
Fine	(Pronounced "feé-nay.") The end. If you see this in the middle of a song, keep going and end at this point when the song repeats.
loco	Resume playing in the octave written..
pizz	Pizzicato (pluck the string with the right forefinger).
↓×	1. Left hand pizzicato. 2. Rhythm part
rit.	(Ritardando) Italian for slow down.
rubato	Slow and rhapsodical. Stretch the long notes and play the short ones very quickly.
simile	Continue playing in the same manner.
Sul A	On the A string.
ten.	Stress the note and hold it out slightly, but not as long as a fermata.
tr	Trill. Folk music trills are generally executed by rocking your hand back and forth to bring the trilling finger into periodic contact with the string. Although usually performed with the note above, they are sometimes (for convenience) performed with the note below.

To the rhythm player(s):

The default rhythm for tunes in 2 is:

The default rhythm for tunes in 6/8, 9/8, or 12/8 is: , etc.

The default rhythm for tunes in 3 (waltz) is: unless otherwise noted.

 = Rhythmic variants for specific parts of a song

Chord symbols:

Letter name only: major (e.g., **A**)

m = minor (e.g., **Am**)

º = diminished (e.g., **Aº**)

+ = augmented (e.g., **A+**)

A numeral after a chord includes the inclusion of that scale degree (e.g,. **A7, A9**)

Δ = major 7 (e.g., **A**Δ)

( ) = alternate chords; e.g.,(**A**)

Tacet = rest

1. Jesuscita in Chihuahua (Jesse Polka)

This Mexican polka was popularized during the Mexican Revolution and subsequently adapted to the Texas fiddle style. It has countless arrangements. This is the way I learned it from Joe Compean, whose family has played mariachi music for generations. The optional D section can be inserted between any two section in G.

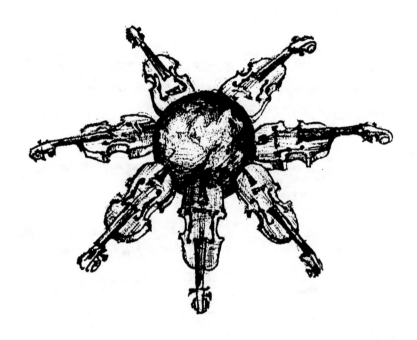

2. Cattle in the Cane

This typical Bluegrass modal tune starts in A mixolidian (A major with a lowered 7th), changing to the parallel minor, A minor. The double stop (playing on two strings at once) unisons and fifths, slides, and Georgia shuffle bowing (♪♪♪ ♪♪♪) are characteristic of this style. (Georgia shuffle places a natural emphasis on the note following the slur.)

Cattle in the Cane

American
Bluegrass Breakdown

3. Blackberry Blossom

This American selection belongs to a genre of fiddle tunes beginning in a major key (in this case G) and going to its relative minor (in this case E minor) in the second part. The first and third beats of the first two measures of the melody are the first four notes of a descending G major scale, the song's trademark. The walking (descending stepwise) bass line continues this.

The bowing is sawstroke (separate bows) and Georgia shuffle. If you accent each note following a slur by using extra bow length and speed you'll soon find yourself at the tip, so there's an extra long slurred upbow at the end of measure 4 to get you back to the frog (compensatory bowing).

Triplets, slides, chromatics (moving by half steps) and an occasional double stop or full chord, ornament the tune. The variation alters the bowing pattern in the first two bars, moving the accent to the first beat of every group of four notes. Since the first note in each group of four must take the same length of bow as the following notes, it will automatically be louder. This brings out the descending scale line formed by those accented notes. Subsequent bowings break up the monotony and facilitate string crossings, etc.

Ricochet, borrowed from the Scottish bag of tricks (see Banks Hornpipe for a description), makes a flashy variation in A¹. The top, repeated note of each arpeggio again delineates the descending G major scale for three measures.

This section segues into a smooth B variation sporting plenty of chromatics, for a slick contest-style wrap up. The hemiola (three-note figure in 4/4 time) 5 bars from the end accents the open E's placing them on the downbows.

Blackberry Blossom

American Bluegrass, Texas-Style
Old-Time Reel

4. Jolie Blon

The eighth notes in this Cajun classic "Pretty Blonde" have a swing dotted feel. This version is a hybrid of a dozen or so traditional renditions, with a typical tag ending on the IV chord. Characteristic devices include the slides, grace notes, triplets, open string drones and other double stops.

Jolie Blon

American Waltz
Cajun

12

5. La Bastringue

We added a harmony to this French Canadian standard. In section B, make the quick back-and-forth string crossings by rocking the bow, crossing strings back and forth while holding the same note on one string. Meanwhile, the notes on the other string can change. For the first and second, fifth and sixth bars of that section hold the A string finger down while you change fingers on the E. Do this around the middle of the bow by making a circular motion from your elbow, keeping your upper arm relatively still.

La Bastringue

French Canadian
Reel

6. La Grande Chaine

The title, translated as "The Big Line," refers to the dance that's done to this tune.

La Grande Chaine

French Canadian
Reel

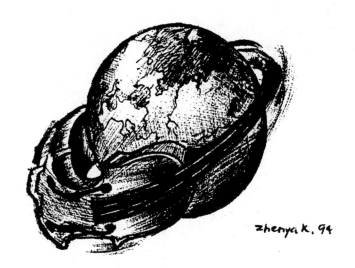

7. St. Anne's Reel

The first time through we present the simple version, followed by the ornamented one. Again, we added harmonies.
In the B sections, the G and E minor chords can be used interchangeably.

St. Anne's Reel

French Canadian
Reel

simile

17

8. Arthritica

After playing this lively Cape Breton B♭ reel we think you'll understand Diehl Moran's title! Accompaniment players, note the walking bass line in the B section.

Arthritica

Cape Breton
Reel

The Irish Tunes

I am grateful to the Houston Irish Session players who contributed their renditions of and recorded the Irish and Shetland tunes for this volume. In addition to the popular jigs and reels we've included less common polkas, slip jigs and a slide, with a new twist - harmonies!

For light and fast articulation of Irish left hand ornaments, the fingers remain close to the strings, barely touching them when they strike.

For Irish grace notes (♪ , ♫), flick the ornamenting finger as though you were touching something hot. When there is a pair of grace notes, this applies to the second one.

The dotted quarter roll (♩.) is a five-note ornament around the main note: ♩. =

The bowed triplet (♫) is played quickly by quivering the wrist so the bow shakes very fast. It can either be a single pitch played three times in a row, or an ornament filling in two skipwise eighth notes with the pitch between them. The first two notes may be quicker than the third.

A note with a slide (╱) often has a slight halt at the end.

9. Coleraine

Play this Irish jig with a dotted feel (♩. ♫).

Coleraine

Irish
Jig

10. Dennis Murphy's Slide

A 12/8 Irish dance.

Dennis Murphy's Slide

Irish
Slide

11. Farewell to Erin

Here are both a simple and an ornamented version of this modal reel. Sections A through C are in A Dorian; Section D is in A Mixolydian. Notice the last measure of every 4-bar phrase but the first is practically the same! Play the eighth notes with a dotted feel. Rhythm players can play an A diad (A and E, no 3rd) instead of major and minor chords, throughout the entire song.

Farewell to Erin 1

Irish
Reel

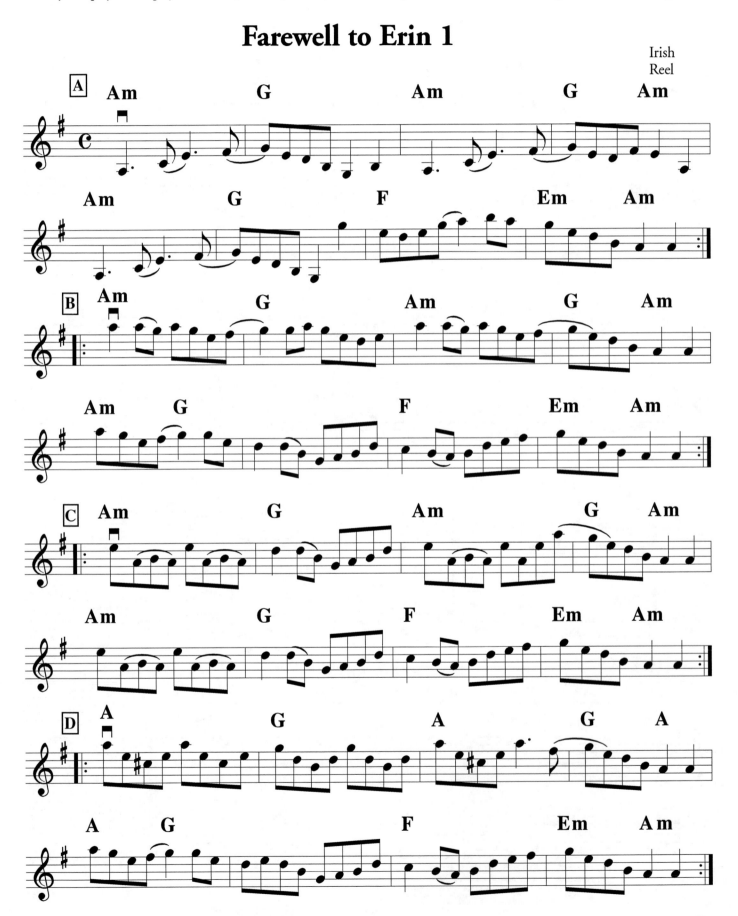

Farewell to Erin 2

Irish
Reel

12. Irish Polka Medley

We thought it would be fun to include a few easy tunes of a less familiar Irish type!

Spanish Ladies

Irish
Polka

24

Sweeny's Polka

Irish
Polka

Dennis Murphy's Polka

Irish
Polka

Lively

26

John Ryan's Polka

Irish
Polka

13. Slip Jig Medley

Accent the first of every three beats. The dotted rhythms give the tune a lilt. The dotted figures can be rolled; e.g.

Fox Hunter's

Irish
Slip Jig

28

Barney Brallaghan's

Irish
Slip Jig

Laura Gibson, champion Irish stepdancer.

14. Tarbolton

Play the eighth notes of this reel with a dotted feel.

Tarbolton

Irish
Reel

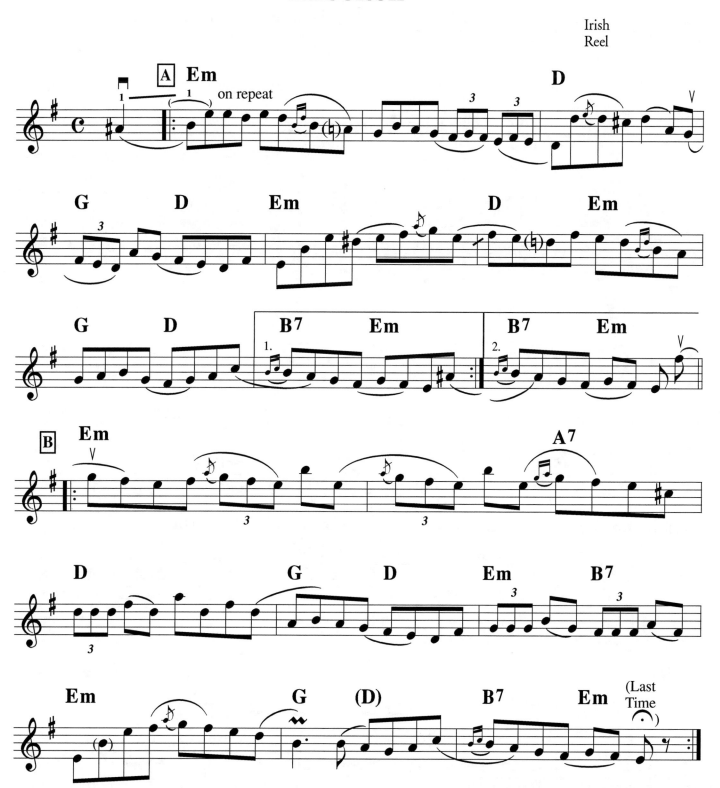

15. Banks Hornpipe

Scottish fiddle music is known for its right hand techniques, such as the ricochet (in this case, fingering a chord on three or four strings while bowing back and forth over them in a slurred, bounced arpeggio) in the B′ section of this hornpipe. The popularity of the flat keys comes from the bagpipe.

The discussion of Irish ornaments applies here as well. Use a crisp stroke on the single bows. Start the ricochet by dropping the upper arm to bounce the bow on the G string from the air on the downbow. Continue dropping the arm to cross over to the E, letting the bow bounce off each string in passing; then reverse.

Banks Hornpipe

Scottish
Hornpipe

32

16. Morpeth Rant

This Northumbrian tune lends itself nicely to harmonization, as presented.

Morpeth Rant

Northumbrian
(Northeast England)
Dance Tune

17. Full-Rigged Ship

Shetland music has a strong Scandinavian influence, which can be felt when you emphasize beat 2 of each bar.

Full-Rigged Ship

Shetland Islands
Reel

18. Gardy Belotin

Play this characteristic Scandinavian tune and the next at moderate tempo. The first and second beats of [A] are punctuated by heavy accents produced by increased bow speed and weight. Open string drones are characteristic of the style; feel free to add them.

Gardy Belotin

Swedish
Walking Tune

19. The Wanderer's Tune

The pointers for the previous number apply here. Scandinavian tunes such as these are commonly played by groups of fiddles. This one includes a typical harmony.

The Wanderer's Tune

Swedish
Folk Dance

20. Clarinet Polka (Dziadek Polka)

Pronounced "Jadek," this Polish polka has been adapted to the American fiddle style and originally dubbed "The Grandfather Polka." The format is: AABBAACCAA.

Dziadek Polka
(Clarinet Polka)

Polish
Polka

21. Fiddler's Polka

This Polish village tune gained popularity as the "Pizzicato Polka" on the Polish-American polka circuit. Pluck the open E with the left hand on the designated notes (⨯). Use a slightly detached bowstroke throughout.

Fiddler's Polka

Polish
Polka

40

22. Krakowiak

This dance comes from the Polish state of Krakow (pronounced "Krá-kov").

Krakowiak

Polish
Krakowiak

23. Ay Lučka Lučka

Pronounced "Ay Loochka Loochka," this Czech tune is played with a somewhat broad, detached stroke.

Ay Lučka Lučka

Czech
Polka

43

24. A Ja Sam

Pronounced "Ay Ya Sahm," this Czech tune is played with a somewhat broad, detached stroke.

A Ja Sam

Czech

25. Tançuj, Tançuj

Pronounced "Tonsoy, Tonsoy," this Slovak tune is played with a somewhat broad, detached stroke.

Tançuj, Tançuj

Slovak

Same rhythm throughout section

Hungarian Czardas Medley

The standard Czardas (pronounced "Char´-dash") has three songs as follows: The first (hallgato) is slow, rubato (stretch the long notes and play the short ones very quickly) ad lib (take your own liberties with the tempo.) The second is a verbunkos ("ver-bun´-kosh"), or military style tune played in march tempo. The third, the friss (pronounced "freesh") takes off at lightening speed and gets as fast as you can manage. If you like this medley, you might enjoy Mel Bay's *Gypsy Violin*.

26. Ennalam Egy Boldog Ora

This particular Hungarian hallgato happens to be favored by German Gypsies as well, for its low, dark sound. Play it rubato ad lib. The squiggly line in the middle of line two indicates a slide with a concurrent vibrato/shake. Roll the A minor chord at the beginning of line four. Rhythm players can hold long notes or tremolo, except where market "tacet" (rest).

Ennalam Egy Boldog Ora

Hungarian
Hallgato

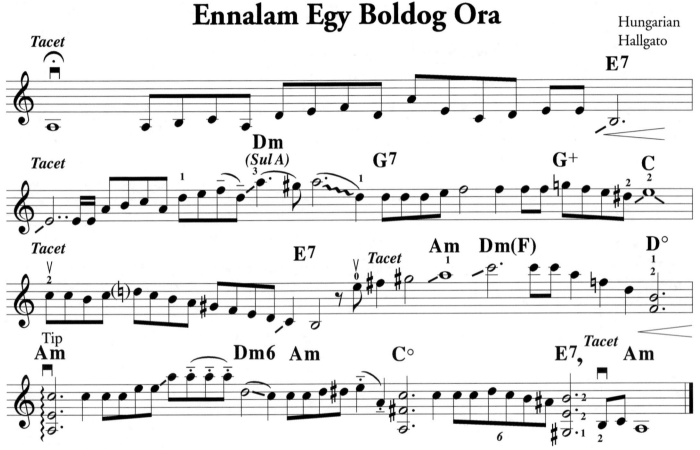

27. Szép Assonynak

Use a short, detached bowstroke for this march-style verbunkos. Rhythm plays on beats one and three.

Szép Assonynak Kurizalok
(Pretty Date)

Hungarian
Verbunkos

28. Vega Vega Mar

Bounce the bow on the quarter notes. Play this friss as fast as you can execute the eighth notes at the end of each section.

Vega Vega Mar

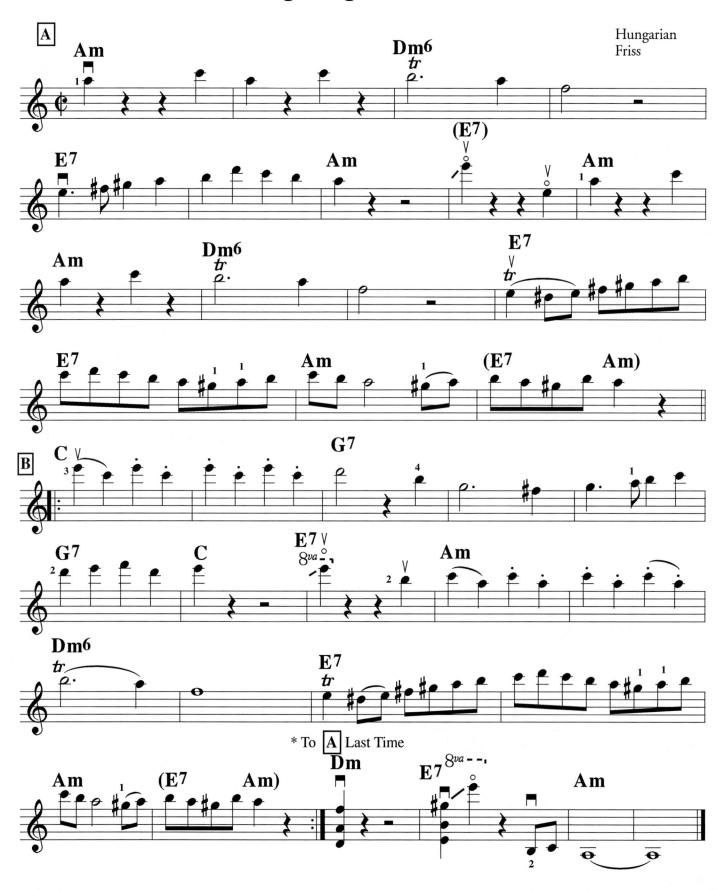

Hungarian
Friss

48

29. Danza Piemontese

Bounce the bow, spiccato. Some of the leads on this and the subsequent two Italian tunes are played by the mandolin and accordion on the companion CD; you can play them just as easily on the violin.

Danza Piemontese

Italian
Polka

30. La Quadriga

Bounce the bow, spiccato. The format is: AABBAACCAA.

La Quadriga

Italian
Square dance

31. Sicilian Tarantella

The melodic rhythm in the first two sections derives from the idiomatic picking of the mandolin so prevalent in Italian music. Use a short, detached stroke on section E.

Sicilian Tarantella

Italian
Tarantella

54

32. Drmeš iz Ždenčine

Bounce the bow. This Drmes (pronounced "Dermish") repeats a fourth higher, a common Croatian device. At the end you can go back to the top, and go through the song as many times as desired.

Drmeš iz Ždencině

Croatian
Drmes

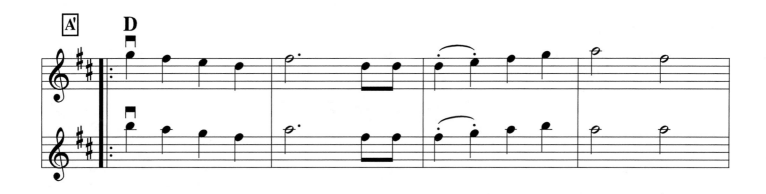

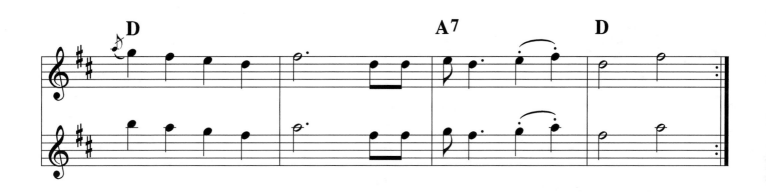

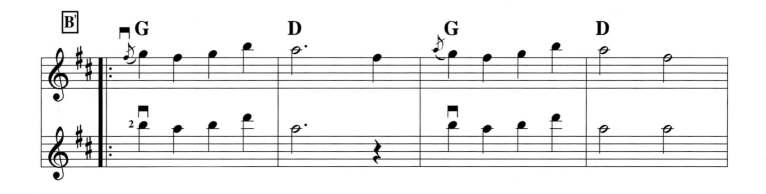

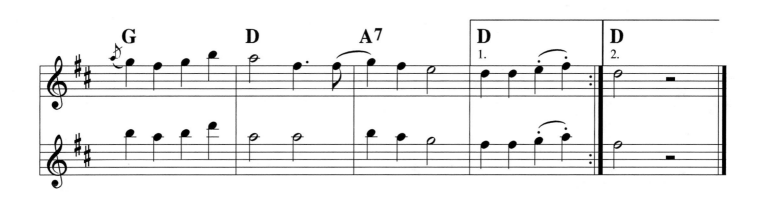

Kolos

These next four tunes are the popular, quick-stepping, arms-interlocked dance known as the kolo. They repeat a fourth or a fifth higher, in typical Serbian form.

33. Čujes Mala

Yes, there really is an F natural over the D7, and C natural over A7 chord on the last line of each page, respectively! And yes, the tune ends on the dominant chord, without resolution! Perhaps it's a reflection of the Balkan political unrest. The title is pronouced "Choo´-yesh Mah´la."

Čujes Mala

Serbian Kolo

Prague, Czechoslovakia

34. Ja Sam Jovicu

Once again, both sections of this spirited kolo ("Ya Sahm Yo-vee-coo") end on the V chord! The A7 with a C♮ in the melody, and the corresponding D7 with F♮ in the melody are typical.

Ja Sam Jovicu

Serbian
Kolo

35. Seljančika

Pronounced "Sel-yan´-chi-ka." Bounce the bow on the quarter notes.

Seljančica

Serbian
Kolo

62

63

36. Užičko

Another typical ending on the dominant chord, and again, bounce the bow. Once more, we have that natural versus sharp third dissonance over the secondary dominant in bar seven of each A section.

Užičo

Serbian
Kolo

37. Hassaposérviko

This dance is a blend of the Greek Hassapiko (Butcher's or Sailor's war dance) and a faster, more driving Serbian folk dance. It's typically played on the long-necked, gourd-shaped bouzouki. Rhythm players, emphasize the offbeat.

The tune is in G harmonic minor and G major, spending a good deal of time on the D7 dominant chord. There it utilizes the D Fraigish scale, a G harmonic minor scale starting on D, resulting in a half step between the first two notes (D and E♭), followed by a minor third from E♭ to F♯, giving it an exotic sound.

The interval of a third is pretty much maintained between the melody and harmony (parallel harmonies in either sixths or thirds are common in Greek music), the harmony being sometimes on top and sometimes underneath.

Hassaposérviko

Greek
Hassapiko

66

38. Karagouna

The A minor scale here sometimes uses the raised fourth (D sharp).

Karagouna

Greek
Karagouna

Fade out

39. Samiotissa

"Samiotissa," (with this authentic harmony) is perhaps the best known and loved kalamatiano, a Greek dance in 7/8. Count this typical 7/8 tune ONE-two-three ONE-two ONE-two (slow, quick quick). The odd time signature accommodates the hopping, skipping dance steps and the leader's various leaps and whirls.

The kalamatiano originated in the town of Kalamata, which produced precious silk scarves. Scarves were an instrument of courtship when it was a scandal to hold hands, spawning the tradition of the leader and the next person in line in Greek dances being joined by a kerchief rather than a handhold.

"Samiotissa" invites a lovely maiden to live on the scenic island of Samos, promising to take her there on a boat with golden sails and oars.

Samiotissa

Greek
Kalamatiano

70

40. Makedonsko Devojke

Count this 7/8 tune praising the beauty of Macedonian girls: ONE-two-three ONE-two ONE-two.

Makedonsko Devojke

Macedonian
Circle Dance

41. Bučimiš

Count this 15/8 rhythm BUM-chick BUM-chick BUM-ch BUM-chick. (The BUM-ch is shorter than the others - three eighth notes as opposed to four.) Rhythm players, note the stops on the first duet section.

Bučimiš

Bulgarian
Line Dance

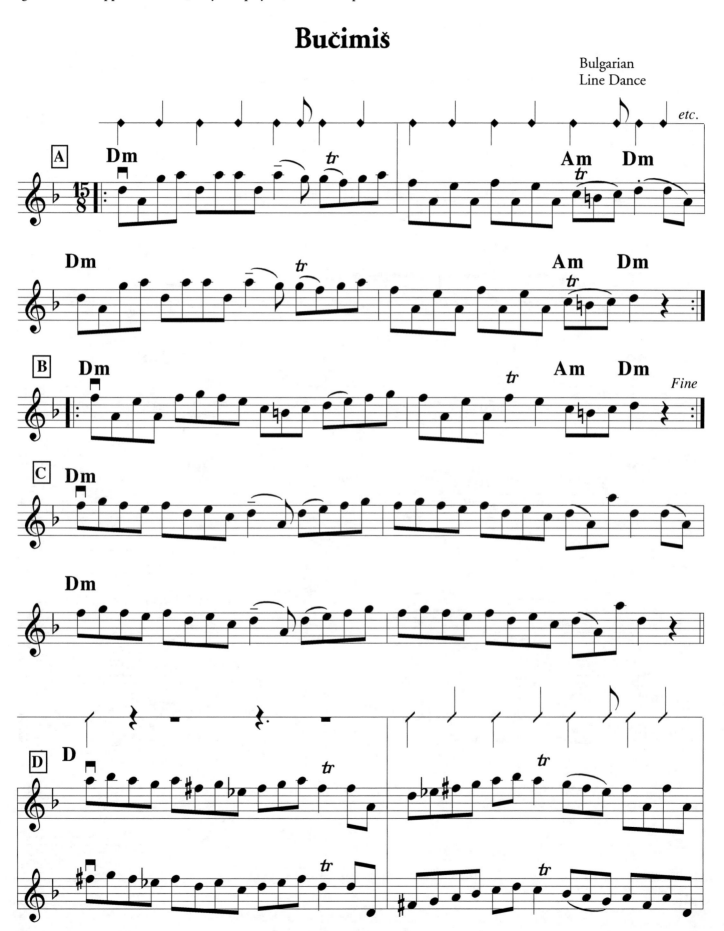

Romanian Set

The Romanians, like the Hungarians, often start a dance or table set slow and end fast, with anywhere from two to half a dozen numbers. We cut to the chase here with a doina followed by Romania's most popular folk violin tune.

42. Doina

You might call this a "mini-doina" - just a taste of the Romanian wailing lament. Note the raised fourth degree (D sharp) prevalent in Romanian minor scales, and the wide interval between it and the third (C natural). Play this piece ad lib, drawing out and repeating the triplets as much as you like. The written timing is very approximate; the rubato style indicates playing the eighth notes quickly and holding out the long notes.

43. The Lark

You can show off on this simplified condensation of Romania's swooping, soaring violin extravaganza. On the companion CD we go straight to the coda; however, bird calls and chirps in the E string stratosphere are traditionally inserted, ad lib, as indicated. If you want to treat yourself, find it on a European folk or Gypsy CD under "Ciocirlia," (its Romanian name), "Pacsirta" (Hungarian), "L'Alouette" (French) "L'Alondra" (Spanish) etc. For a discussion of kontra (backup violin) as on the recording, see Mel Bay's *Gypsy Violin*.

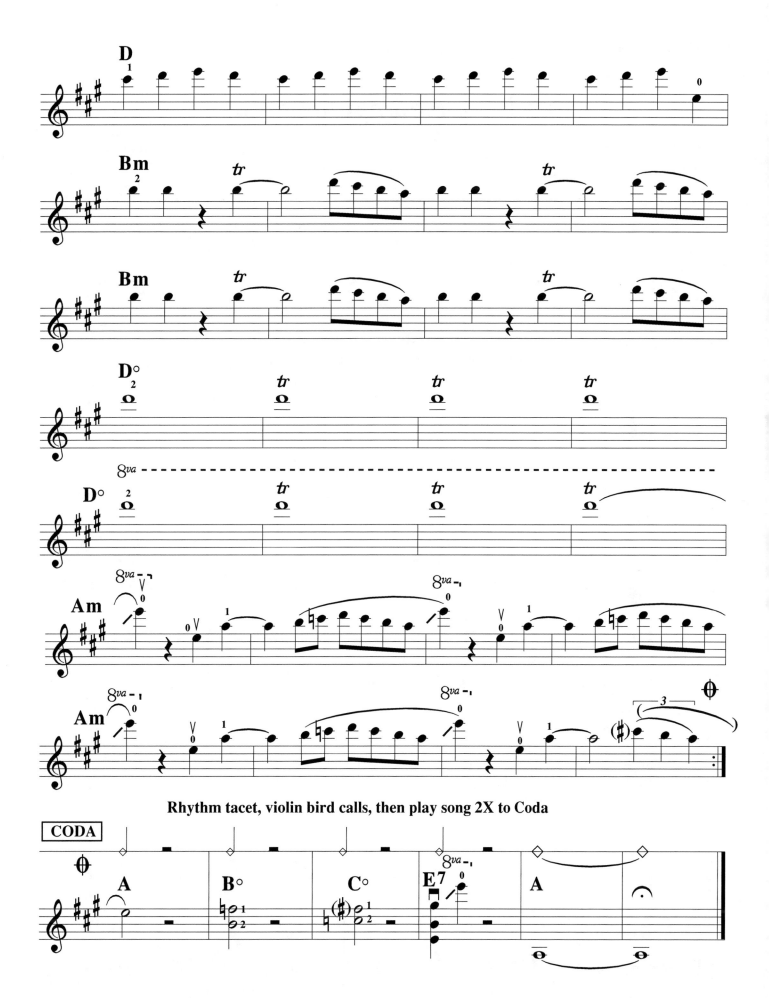

Rhythm tacet, violin bird calls, then play song 2X to Coda

44. Slow Hora in D Minor

Not to be confused with the waltz, the Moldavian hora places the accents on beats one and three.

Hora Mare A Cîmpulungului

Moldavian
Circle Dance

Romanian Band

45. 7:40 A.M.

The title of this klezmer number refers to a train that someone took to work every morning. Bounce the bow on section A, and play the tune with plenty of spirit.

Seven-Forty A.M.

Jewish
Frailach

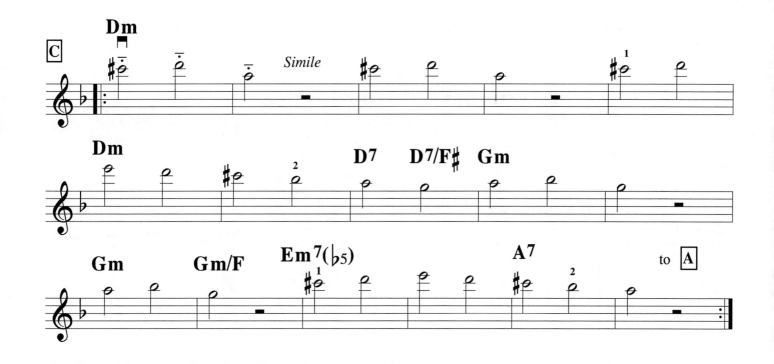

46. Klezmer Wedding Dance

This tune came out on a CD by Muzikas; we took the liberty of harmonizing it. Use a short, articulated bowstroke.

Klezmer Wedding Dance

Jewish
Dance

47. Kolomeyka Medley

Play these lively Ukrainian dances fast and crisp, using mostly a bounced or separated stroke.
Our longtime friend and occasional bass balalaika player Steve Wolownik's godfather, Michael Edynack, wrote the Boyko Kolomeyka (Song #3). This dance form is very much alive and well in the Ukraine today.

Kolomeyka Medley
Song #1

Ukrainian
Kolomeyka

Song #2

Ukrainian
Kolomeyka

Song #3

Ukrainian
Kolomeyka

48. Ukrainian Medley

Arkan is a show-off tune for male dancers, with plenty of leaps, knee-slapping and other flashy calisthenics. Start slow for the warm-up and repeat Arkan as many times as you want, accelerating throughout. Play the opening passage on two strings at once, avoiding the E string with your left hand, to sound the open E drones. You can do the third finger trill in measure eleven by shaking your hand. Play these selections with a crisp feel as in the previous medley, bouncing the bow where possible.

Arkan

Ukrainian
Men's Line Dance

Tuzhe Mene

Ukrainian
Folk Song

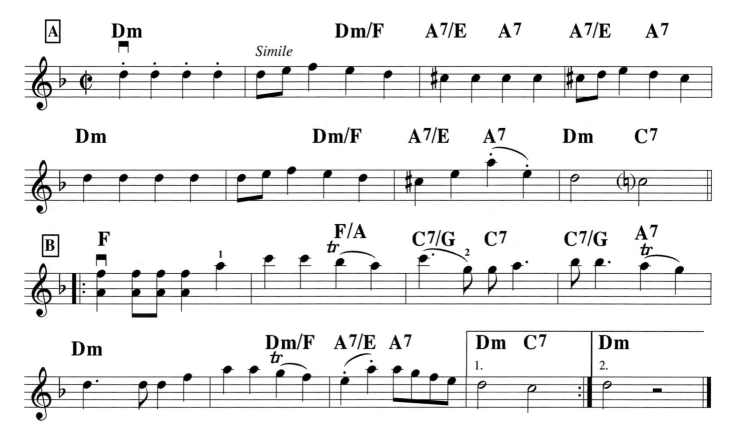

Komar

Ukrainian
Folk Song

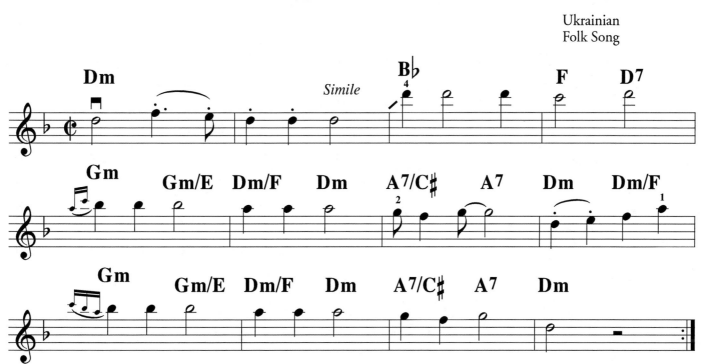

49. Kolomeyka#1

This spirited Ukrainian dance is among our favorites - we've put some parties to bed with this one! Don't confuse the title with the first kolomeyka in selection #47; this one's just at the top of our personal list. That's my Byelorussian husband Greg wailing on the accordion on the CD -pardon my enthusiasm - Bounce the bow wherever you see a dot over a notehead.

Kolomeyka #1

Ukrainian
Kolomeyka

86

50. Musician's Polka

We got a little carried away with the tempo on this one, for a polka, but how can one help it with this music?

Musician's Polka

Ukrainian
Polka

Ukrainian Orchestra

51. Hopak

Another men's show-off dance. You can bounce the bow, especially on section B. C and D are played over and over while the dancers leap, twirl, do the kazatzkis and otherwise amaze the audience.

Hopak

Ukrainian
Men's Dance

91

52. Bright Shines the Moon

This arrangement is taken from the Andreyev variations played by Russian balalaika orchestras for as long as anyone can remember. The first variation is traditionally played by the bass balalaika (you can hear it on the CD), but you can play it as written, plucked or bowed, on the violin. Bounce the bow on the quarter notes.

Bright Shines the Moon

Russian
Folk Song

94

95

VARIATION 4

53. Karapyet

Also known as "Dyevoutchke Nadia" or "The Russian Two-Step," this song is about an attractive young woman. It was adopted by the Polish-American community as "Who Stole the Kishka?", expounding upon that sausage in such terms as "round, firm, fully packed"... need we say more?

Use an articulated stroke. You could trill the B flat in the second bar of B2 with the lower finger. The first variation was adapted from one my Byelorussian husband Greg invented on the accordion.

Karapyet

Russian
Couple Dance

97

VARIATION 1

54. Korobushka

Use an articulated stroke for this dance "The Peddler's Pack." Bounce the bow for the quarter notes in the arco sections. The second variation is a bass (balalaika) solo. Under the third variation, violin two plays the original folk melody.

Korobushka

Russian
Couple Dance

VARIATION 1

101

104

55. Leyla

We've played this slow, tantalizing number for many a belly dancer. Note the wide interval between the F natural and G sharp.

Leyla

Middle Eastern
Rhumba oriental

* Basic rhythm:

105

56. Aziz

Another belly dance favorite, this tune employs the Fraigish scale - G harmonic minor played from D to D over D7. Take care on the F# to E♭ interval in line two. You can improvise while your rhythm section holds a D7.

Aziz

Middle Eastern
Balady
(Belly Dance)

57. Mustafa

If you live in a cosmopolitan area, chances are the fellow behind the counter at your local gas station or convenience store will know this one. It uses that exotic harmonic minor scale with the raised fourth in section B. The form is played: Intro - A - Intro - B - Intro. Watch for the key change at letter B.

Mustafa

Arabic
Balady

58. Omni

And now for something contemporary! This piece was inspired by our camping experience with the Gypsies at the Django Reinhardt Festival in Samois-sur-Seine, France. Improvisation is the wellspring of music. It seems fitting to end this volume by returning the joy of creating to you, the musician. You can begin by arpeggiating over the plain, unaltered major, minor and dominant 7th chords for this song and then move ahead as you please. We've laid down a violin melody and guitar break (both of which you can eliminate using your balance control) on the companion CD and the last chorus is an additional rhythm track for your own solos.

Omni

Manouche Sinti
Gypsy Style Bossa
Mary Ann Harbar

Photo by Rick Gardner

Alphabetical Index of Titles

7:40 A.M.	78	Karapyet	97
A Ja Sam	44	Klezmer Wedding Dance	80
Arthritica	19	Kolomeyka Medley	81
Arkan	84	Kolomeyka #1	86
Ay Lučka Lučka	43	Komar	85
Aziz	106	Korobushka	100
Banks Hornpipe	32	Krakowiak	42
Barney Brallaghan's	29	La Bastringue	13
Blackberry Blossom	10	La Grande Chaine	14
Bright Shines the Moon	92	La Quadriga	52
Bučimiš	72	Leyla	105
Cattle in the Cane	9	Makedonsko Devojke	71
Clarinet Polka	38	Morpeth Rant	34
Coleraine	20	Musician's Polka	88
Čujes Mala	58	Mustafa	107
Danza Piemontese	50	Omni	108
Dennis Murphy's Polka	26	Samiotissa	70
Dennis Murphy's Slide	21	Seljančika	62
Doina	74	Sicilian Tarantella	54
Drmeš iz Żdenčine	56	Slip Jig Medley	28
Ennalam Egy Boldog Ora	46	Slow Hora in D Minor	76
Farewell to Erin	22	Spanish Ladies	24
Fiddler's Polka	40	St. Anne's Reel	16
Fox Hunter's	28	Sweeny's Polka	25
Full-Rigged Ship	35	Szép Assonynak	46
Gardy Belotin	36	Tançuj, Tançuj	45
Hassaposérviko	66	Tarbolton	31
Hopak	90	The Lark	74
Ja Sam Jovicu	61	The Wanderer's Tune	37
Jesuscita in Chihuahua (Jesse Polka)	6	Tuzhe Mene	85
John Ryan's Polka	27	Ukrainian Medley	84
Jolie Blon	12	Užičko	64
Karagouna	69	Vega Vega Mar	48

About the Author

Mary Ann Harbar earned her Bachelor's degree and teaching credential in music from the University of California, with finishing studies in Switzerland and Italy. Since that time she has apprenticed with folk fiddlers of many nationalities, in addition to extensive transcriptions and studies from performances and recordings. She and her husband Greg have entertained international audiences studded with royalty, heads of state, and stars with their Houston, TX, band The Gypsies.

Photo by Rick Gardner